GOVERNMENTS AND LEADERS

of the Middle East

David Downing

Academic Consultant:
William Ochsenwald
Professor of History, Virginia Polytechnic Institute
and State University

WORLD ALMANAC® LIBRARY

Please visit our website at: www.garethstevens.com
For a free color catalog describing World Almanac® Library's list of high-quality books
and multimedia programs, call 1-800-848-2928 (USA) or 1-800-387-3178 (Canada).
World Almanac® Library's Fax: (414) 332-3567.

Library of Congress Cataloging-in-Publication Data

Downing, David, 1946-
    Governments and leaders of the Middle East / David Downing.
        p. cm. — (World Almanac Library of the Middle East)
    Includes bibliographical references and index.
    ISBN-10: 0-8368-7335-1 — ISBN-13: 978-0-8368-7335-1 (lib. bdg.)
    ISBN-10: 0-8368-7342-4 — ISBN-13: 978-0-8368-7342-9 (softcover)
    1. Middle East—Juvenile literature. I. Title. II. Series.
    DS44.D68   2006
    956—dc22   2006014030

First published in 2007 by
World Almanac® Library
A Member of the WRC Media Family of Companies
330 West Olive Street, Suite 100
Milwaukee, WI 53212, USA

Produced by Discovery Books
Editors: Geoff Barker, Amy Bauman, Paul Humphrey, and Sarah Jameson
Series designer: Sabine Beaupré
Designer and page production: Ian Winton
Photo researchers: Sarah Jameson and Rachel Tisdale
Maps and diagrams: Stefan Chabluk and Ian Winton
Academic Consultant: William Ochsenwald,
    Professor of History, Virginia Polytechnic Institute and
    State University
World Almanac® Library editorial direction: Mark J. Sachner
World Almanac® Library editor: Alan Wachtel
World Almanac® Library art direction: Tammy West
World Almanac® Library production: Jessica Morris

Photo credits: cover: Markus Matzel/Still Pictures; p. 5: Wathiq Khuzaie/Getty Images;
p. 7: General Photographic Agency/Hulton Archive/Getty Images; p. 8: Hulton Archive/
Getty Images; p. 10: Khaled Al-Sayyed/AFP/Getty Images; p. 12: AFP/Getty Images; p. 15:
Ronald Startup/Picture Post/Getty Images; p. 16: © Bettmann/CORBIS; p. 19:
Keystone/Getty Images; p. 20: Central Press/Getty Images; p.22: Bob Landry/Time Life
Pictures/Getty Images; p. 25: Keystone/Getty Images; p. 26: Keystone/Getty Images; p. 28:
Quique Kierszenbaum/Getty Images; p. 29: Ron Sachs/Consolidated News/Getty Images;
p. 30: Will Yurman/Getty Images; p. 32: Mauricio Lima/AFP/Getty Images; p. 34: Hulton
Archive/Getty Images; p. 36: Faleh Kheiber/AFP/Getty Images; p. 39: Karim
Sahib/AFP/Getty Images; p. 41: David Silverman/Getty Images; p. 42: U.S. Marine
Corps/Lance Cpl. Michael J. O'Brien.

Printed in the United States of America

1 2 3 4 5 6 7 8 9 10 09 08 07 06

CONTENTS

Cover: *U.S. troops pull down the huge, bronze statue of Saddam Hussein in Al-Ferdous square, Baghdad, in April 2003.*

The Middle East

The term *Middle East* has a long and complex history. It was originally used by the British in the nineteenth century to describe the area between the Near East (those lands gathered around the eastern end of the Mediterranean Sea) and Britain's empire in India. This area included Persia (later Iran), the **Mesopotamian provinces** of the **Ottoman Empire** (later Iraq), and the eastern half of Saudi Arabia. It was centered on the Persian Gulf.

In this series, the Middle East is taken to include the following fifteen countries: Libya and Egypt in north Africa, along with Israel, Lebanon, Syria, Jordan, Iraq, and Iran, and

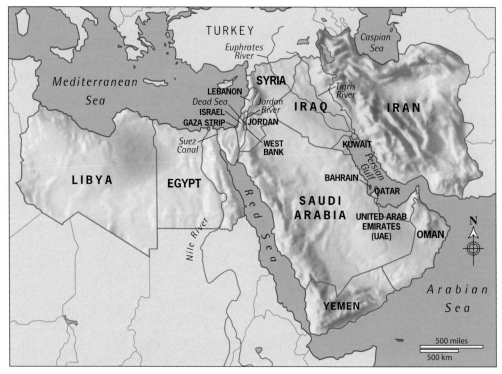

This map shows the fifteen countries of the Middle East that will be discussed in this book, as well as the West Bank and the Gaza Strip.

An Iraqi woman casts her vote in Iraq's December 2005 elections. The installation of democratic government in Iraq has so far proved the most notable achievement of the country's foreign occupiers.

the **Arabian peninsula** countries of Bahrain, Kuwait, Saudi Arabia, United Arab Emirates (UAE), Oman, Yemen, and Qatar. It also includes the disputed Arab Palestinian territories—the West Bank and Gaza Strip—which have had varying degrees of autonomy under Israeli occupation since 1967.

Why is this region important? Two reasons stand out. One, the Middle East was the original source of civilization, and the three great religions of Christianity, **Judaism**, and **Islam** all grew up there. The area includes Israel, the state of the Jewish people, and a significant proportion of the world's **Muslims**. Two, the Middle East has two-thirds of the fuel that keeps the rest of the world running—oil.

For these two reasons alone, the affairs of the Middle East—its peoples and resources, religions and politics, revolutions and wars—are of vital interest to everyone on the planet. This book looks at the governments and leaders of the Middle East. A look at the legacies of the Ottoman Empire and Anglo-French **colonialism** is followed by an examination of the different types of government that characterize the modern region. Evaluating potential for greater **democracy**, and the role of outside powers is discussed. The book concludes with a look at the prospects for future government and leadership throughout the region.

CHAPTER 1

The Legacy of the Past

In the seventh and eighth centuries, Arab military power and Arab eagerness to spread the new religion of Islam combined to create an empire that stretched from the Atlantic Ocean to modern-day Afghanistan. For most of the next five hundred years, much of the Middle East was ruled by Middle Easterners. Between the mid-thirteenth and mid-twentieth centuries, however, the region was mostly ruled by outsiders: the Mongols, the Ottoman Turks, the British, and the French. All of these rulers left their mark on the region, and the Ottoman and Anglo-French periods in particular continue to influence the governments and leaders that rule today's Middle East.

The Ottoman Legacy

During the time of the Arab empire, there was a close connection between political and religious leadership. This continued after the conquest of the Middle East by the Muslim Ottoman Turks. The Ottoman emperor had two roles: that of **sultan** and that of **caliph**. As sultan, he was the Ottoman Empire's political leader; as caliph he claimed to be the religious leader of all Muslims, both inside and outside his empire. The caliphate survived the fall of the Ottoman Empire but was finally abolished in the early 1920s. But even today, because of the long-standing connection between politics and religion, the idea that religion should play a role in government seems much more normal to many people in the Middle East than it does in North America or most of Europe, where a long tradition of separating government and religion exists.

Winston Churchill, then the British Colonial Secretary, attended the 1921 Cairo Conference in Egypt. British authorities from all over the Middle East were present at this conference, which had been called to decide the future of the region.

The last one hundred years of Ottoman rule saw attempts to **modernize** the empire. This modernization involved the adoption of European ideas and practices such as **nationalism** and efficient administration. But the Ottoman leaders made no serious attempt to introduce democracy. They had no intention of allowing their Arab and other non-Turkish subjects any real say in how they were governed. So when the Turks were finally ejected from the Middle East in 1918 at the end of World War I, the Arab peoples had little preparation for self-rule.

The Anglo-French Legacy

But even before this, new powers were coming into play in the Middle East—namely Britain and France. By the end of the nineteenth century, Britain controlled Egypt and exerted a controlling influence in the Persian Gulf area. In World War I, the Turks sided with Germany, and after their joint defeat Ottoman rule in the Middle East was replaced by British and French rule. The **League of Nations** granted Britain **mandates** to rule Palestine (which then included the future Transjordan) and Iraq, and France a mandate to rule Syria (which included the future Lebanon). The two colonial powers were supposed to prepare these countries for self-rule. Many historians believe, however, that Britain and France put their own interests before the needs of the mandate territories.

The British and French were mainly concerned with safeguarding the sea-routes that connected their homelands to their Indian and Indo-Chinese empires and securing the lion's share of the region's new source of wealth—oil. The main threat to their interests was any sort of **radical** change, so they created **constitutions** and parliaments in their mandate territories that made radical change unlikely. Elections had many stages and were carefully managed to produce parliaments made up of the local pro-Western elite. The British also introduced **constitutional monarchies** but gave the naturally conservative monarchs the power to obstruct any attempt by the parliaments to make significant changes.

The Middle Eastern monarchs and their parliaments often felt frustrated by their foreign masters, but they soon got used to the idea that government was all about holding on to power and making themselves richer. From the example set by their British and French rulers, these Middle Easterners learned that

The future King Faisal of Iraq (then King of Syria) at the Paris Peace Conference in 1919. His liaison officer, the British soldier T. E. Lawrence (Lawrence of Arabia), stands behind his left shoulder.

looking democratic was much more important than actually being democratic. But for the majority of ordinary people in the Middle East these arrangements offered very little. They hungered for economic and political progress, but under these arrangements, none seemed possible. Between the 1920s and the 1950s, then, many people in the Middle East came to believe that democracy and its pro-Western supporters were the main obstacles to the progress in the region.

Musical Kings

From the tenth century, the al Hashem family—often known as the Hashemites—ruled all or part of the Hejaz area of the western Arabian Peninsula. During World War I, Sharif Hussein, the then head of the family, agreed to support the British in their war against the Ottoman Turks. In return, he expected the kingship of a yet-to-be-defined, independent, Arab country. Two of Sharif Hussein's sons did eventually become kings but not of countries they or their father expected.

After the Turks had been driven out of the future Syrian capital, Damascus, in 1918, Faisal, the son of Hussein, set about establishing an independent Arab government. One year later, the local **Arab nationalists** invited him to become king of Syria. Unfortunately for Faisal, Syria was one of the mandate territories that the League of Nations had placed under French control, and the French did not want him as king. The British came to the rescue. They offered Faisal the kingship of Iraq as a way of lessening the intense Iraqi opposition to their mandate. In the meantime, Faisal's younger brother Abdullah had set out to save him from the French. Abdullah and his army reached Transjordan, at which point the British offered to make him ruler of the area if he promised not to invade Syria.

Sharif Hussein controlled the Hejaz area until he was driven out by the Saud family in 1924, and Faisal's grandson, Faisal II, who was then in power in Iraq, was murdered during the Iraqi revolution of 1958. Abdullah's great-grandson, Abdullah II, is still on the throne of Jordan.

CHAPTER 2

Emirs, Shahs, Sultans, and Kings

Where They Came From

The kings who Britain introduced into Egypt and Iraq after World War I were not **dictators**. Their authority was balanced by the authority of newly created parliaments, was constrained by the British, or both. Outside of the mandate areas, however, the situation was very different. In Iran and those parts of the Arabian

Saudi Crown Prince Abdullah (third from left) attends a traditional sword dance ceremony with other members of the royal family in Riyadh, Saudi Arabia, in 2001.

Peninsula that had not been part of the Ottoman Empire, single rulers were the norm. These rulers had many titles—king, **shah**, sultan, **emir**—but all were essentially dictators.

Iran introduced elections and the idea of a parliament in 1907, but by the end of World War I, the country was nearly bankrupt. The British stepped in, replacing parliamentary rule with a strong military leader, Reza Shah, in 1921. He appointed himself shah and ruled as a dictator until Britain and her World War II ally Russia overthrew him for being too pro-German in 1941. His son, who was installed in his place, proved equally dictatorial. He was overthrown by the Iranian Revolution of 1979.

"Among twelve slaves presented to foreign journalists, some had been forced, under pain of beating, not to speak. As a result, they had become mutes. Others stood with their heads bowed and eyes fixed on the ground, their necks now paralyzed. The slightest glance sideways resulted in a severe beating or imprisonment. Others had incurred physical deformity from similar cruelty."

Omani journalist Said Seif, describing the scene in Sultan Said's Salala palace after the sultan's removal, following the British-organized coup of 1970. Quoted in Fred Halliday's Arabia Without Sultans *[New York: Penguin, 1974].*

Powerful Families

The small kingdoms of the Persian Gulf—which eventually became the countries of Kuwait, Bahrain, Qatar, the United Arab Emirates, and Oman—were founded and ruled by powerful, individual families. Kuwait, for example, was taken over by the al-Sabah family in the eighteenth century. The al-Khalifa family in Bahrain and the al-Thani family in Qatar have controlled these kingdoms since the 1780s and 1860s, respectively. In the second half of the nineteenth century, these families guaranteed their continued rule by making deals with the British. The British promised to keep these important families in power in return for naval bases, trading opportunities, and stable governments in their respective territories.

The center of the Arabian Peninsula was conquered by one family—the Saud family—between the two world wars. The state of Saudi Arabia was officially established in 1932. Like the Gulf kingdoms, it was a family dictatorship.

How Family Dicatorships Ruled

How did these family dictatorships work? In most ways, they were remarkably similar to the kingdoms of ancient and medieval Europe. The head of the family had **absolute power**. He—and in the Islamic Middle East the leader was always male—could do whatever he wished with his kingdom and his people.

In Saudi Arabia, for example, the royal family now consists of around 22,000 people, and about 4,000 of these people are princes. These princes hold all of the highest positions in government and the military. The royal family sets the rules of life for all Saudi citizens, using their own religious traditions and beliefs as a guide. These rules derive from **Wahhabism**, the strict version of Islam that played a key role in the family's original rise to power. People in Saudi Arabia have severely limited freedom of expression and behavior. Saudi women, in particular, have lives that are highly restricted by

Muhammad Reza Pahlavi, the shah of Iran, photographed in October 1971 at Persepolis. Huge tents were erected among the ancient ruins for a celebration of 2,500 years of the Iranian monarchy. It lasted only eight more years.

Celebrating Power

In October 1971, the shah of Iran organized a lavish and extravagant celebration of 2,500 years of "unbroken" monarchy at the ancient Persian capital of Persepolis. The main aim of the event was to demonstrate the lasting importance of monarchy to Persia/Iran. It is estimated that nearly 2.5 billion people watched the event on television as the Iranian military paraded through the ruins and numerous visiting heads of state watched in person. The seating was arranged with monarchs at the front and mere presidents at the rear. The guests were housed in luxury tented apartments featuring marble bathrooms. Their meals were flown in from Maxim's restaurant in Paris. Ordinary Iranians were not allowed to attend.

Western standards. They are not permitted to vote, drive a car, or hold any public office. They are only allowed to work in certain jobs, such as teaching or nursing and must not travel unaccompanied on buses or trains.

In Iran, the two shahs took little notice of the wishes and aspirations of their subjects. Reza Shah, who ruled from 1925 to 1941, launched a full-scale attack on the Islamic **clergy**, extending his persecution to ordinary citizens. Many Iranian women, for example, believed that wearing veils over their faces was an essential part of their religion, but when Reza Shah came to power, he ordered his police to tear them off. His son Muhammad Reza Shah Pahlavi spent millions on self-glorification and modern weaponry. In Oman, Sultan Said bin Taimur (1932–1970) isolated his country from the rest of the world and spent the last twelve years of his reign surrounded by slaves and a huge harem of young women.

These rulers were not **accountable** to their subjects. The only real restriction on their behavior was the fear of fellow family members. Some of these family members might think they could do the job better; some might simply be hungry for power. A trusted few were likely to have forces under their control—there was no way the ruler could do everything himself.

Reasons for Their Survival

How have these family dictatorships managed to survive into the twenty-first century? Two main reasons have made their survival possible. The first is wealth. Most of the countries discussed above have enormous reserves of oil. Over the last half-century, the profits from oil sales has been high enough to provide most people in the smaller Gulf kingdoms with a reasonable quality of life. It is as if the family dictators of these countries have made a bargain with their people: "Leave us in power, and we'll share our wealth with you." Among the oil-rich countries, Iran and Saudi Arabia have much bigger populations, so the distribution of oil profits has not made the same difference to most ordinary people. The second shah of Iran was overthrown in part because his country's oil wealth had failed to improve the lives of most Iranians.

The second reason for the survival of the family dictatorships is foreign support. The British protected the Gulf kingdoms into the 1970s and sent troops to help defeat a popular rebellion in Oman. Britain and the United States acted together in 1953 to remove the elected parliamentary leader Mohammed Mossadegh and reinstate the second shah of Iran. The latter's increasing dependence on help from the United States was one of the reasons for his overthrow.

The Saud family were reluctant to deal with the British, and when it needed a partner in oil exploitation it chose the United States. After World War II, the United States began playing the same role in Saudi Arabia that Britain had long played in Egypt, Iraq, and the Gulf. Having decided that a stable Saudi Arabia was essential to its national interests, U.S. leaders made it clear that they would act to protect the Saud family dictatorship. The United States has maintained an almost continuous military presence in the kingdom since World War II.

Over the last few years, an apparent contradiction has arisen between, on the one hand, U.S. support for Saudi Arabia and other family dictatorships and, on the other hand, the Bush administration's stated aim of making the whole Middle East more democratic. A steady process of democratization is possible, but the current uncertainties affecting the region have increased the difficulties and dangers of such a transition.

King Hussein of Jordan

Over the last fifty years, Jordan has been the only oil-poor country in the Middle East to retain a monarchy. The survival of the monarchy was largely due to the political skill and flexibility of King Hussein, who came to the throne in 1952 at the age of seventeen and reigned until his death in 1999. He managed to stay on good terms with the West, guessing, probably correctly, that it would not allow his forcible overthrow by anti-Western Arab nationalists or **Islamists**. At the same time, he tried not to antagonize those Arab groups and nations who opposed Western policy in the Middle East. His expulsion of the Palestinian fighters from Jordan in 1970–1971 brought him temporary unpopularity beyond his kingdom, but the act probably increased his popularity at home. Domestically, he kept power mostly in his own hands but allowed Jordan's parliament enough scope to avoid a build-up of frustration. It remains to be seen whether his son, King Abdullah II, will prove as successful.

The young King Hussein of Jordan, accompanied by his youngest brother and two-year-old sister, shortly after his coronation in May 1953. He occupied the throne for forty-seven years.

CHAPTER 3

One-Party Countries

By the middle of the twentieth century, some Middle Eastern countries had endured long decades of colonial and mandate rule. In these countries two main opposition movements appeared. Both movements would eventually become governments of independent states.

The first movement, led by professional soldiers, was known as the **Free Officers Movement**. This was founded by Colonel Gamal Abdul Nasser of Egypt in 1948. Nasser later became

President Nasser of Egypt addresses Air Force cadets during the **Suez Crisis** in September 1956. Egyptians, he said, would defend their rights to the canal "to the last drop of our blood."

Eygpt's president in 1956. In several countries, groups of young officers, resentful of continued foreign influence and angry at their governments' inability to end it, came together with the intention of seizing power. In both Egypt (1952) and Iraq (1958), the movement proved successful. Power was seized by force of arms, and the existing pro-Western governments were abolished. British power and influence was brought to an end.

The second movement was the **Ba'ath**. This Arabic word means "revival," and the movement was begun by a Syrian teacher, Michel Aflaq, in the 1940s. His and others' writings inspired the creation of Ba'athist parties in many Arab countries. In Syria (1963) and Iraq (1968), these parties came to power.

There was not much difference between the Syrian and Iraqi Ba'ath movements, and they shared many of the same ideas. In some cases, they seemed tangled together—in Syria, for example, many of the leading Ba'athists were young army and air force officers. And in general, members and leaders of both movements were Arab nationalists who believed in unifying and modernizing the Arab world. Most claimed to be democrats but admitted that democracy was not high on their list of priorities.

An Arab Nationalist Definition of Democracy

"**First**. Political democracy cannot be separated from social democracy. No citizen can be regarded as free to vote unless he is given the following three guarantees.

1. He should be free from exploitation in all its forms.

2. He should have an equal opportunity with his fellow citizen to enjoy a fair share of the national wealth.

3. His mind should be free from all anxiety likely to undermine his future security.

Second. Political democracy cannot exist under the domination of any one class. Democracy means, literally, the domination and sovereignty of the people, the whole people."

This definition, taken from the Egyptian National Charter introduced in 1962, shows that Arab nationalists like Nasser held political views that supported one-party rule. As quoted in Peter Mansfield's Nasser's Egypt *[New York: Penguin, 1965].*

Disregarding Democracy

To Arab nationalists, there were several reasons for not being devoted to democracy. They had spent several decades criticizing the ineffectiveness of the parliaments that the British and French had given them. These parliaments seemed more like clubs for the local elite than institutions for organizing change, and they had discredited democracy in the eyes of many ordinary Arabs. As ruling bodies they had proved incapable of getting rid of the foreigners or of doing very much for the poor. They seemed to be all talk, and what the Arab nationalists wanted was action.

Another reason for their lack of devotion to democracy was that Arab nationalists who won real independence for their countries were usually part of one movement or party. That party or movement assumed it had the right to rule the new state that it had brought into being. The idea of more than one party forming the government—an idea that all real democracies share—seemed absurd.

Thirdly, and more importantly as time went by, the new Arab nationalist rulers came to see opposition as obstruction. Anyone who genuinely wanted to see his or her country progress, these rulers felt, should help the government, not hinder it. It was better, they believed, to have an undemocratic leadership that governed in the interests of the people than a democratic government that governed in the interests of foreigners and the rich.

So when President Nasser of Egypt introduced a new constitution in 1956, room was only made for one party, the National Union. Nasser and future presidents would have to seek public approval every six years, but rival parties would have no opportunity to contest power. What debate there was would take place inside the National Union. The Egyptian people were asked to accept or reject this constitution. They voted "yes."

Democracy: An Empty Shell

In the situation that these new governments found themselves, this lack of attention to democracy was not surprising. They knew they had the support of the vast majority of their people and thought nothing could be gained by deliberately encouraging the opposition that democracy needs to thrive.

Hosni Mubarak

Muhammad Hosni Mubarak was born in a Nile Delta village in 1928. After graduating from the Egyptian air force academy in 1950, he served for four years as a fighter pilot. A series of promotions culminated in 1969 with his appointment as air force chief of staff. In 1975, President Anwar Sadat made Mubarak vice-president. When Sadat was **assassinated** in 1981, Mubarak succeeded him as president and as chairman of the ruling National Democratic Party. He maintained Sadat's close alliance with the United States, whose economic aid was crucial to Egypt's economic survival, and upheld the peace deal Sadat had made with Israel. He was reelected, without opposition, in 1987, 1993, and 1999. In 2005, he defeated several other candidates, but the election's fairness was questioned by both Egyptian opponents and outside observers.

Hosni Mubarak, who became president of Egypt after the assassination of Anwar Sadat in 1981, has retained the position ever since.

As the 1960s and 1970s went by, however, this situation changed. Arab nationalism was discredited by a lack of economic success at home and failure to achieve its goal of forcing Israel to withdraw from the occupied Palestinian territories.

Opposition to Arab nationalist governments grew. At the same time, the men who made up these governments grew accustomed to the responsibilities, comforts, and privileges of power, and they were reluctant to give them up. They grew even less tolerant of opposition. Elections were still held, but they meant less and less. Prominent opposition leaders were jailed, and opposition parties were banned. The government wrote the election rules, controlled the election process, and usually

In March 1970, Saddam Hussein (right), who was then deputy chairman of Iraq's ruling Revolutionary Council, held up the hand of Kurdish leader Mustafa Barzani (left), during a period of truce between the two groups.

restricted the information available to the public through newspapers, radio, and TV. When frustrated opponents took to the streets, they were met with overwhelming force. In the Syrian town of Hama, for example, government security forces killed more than five thousand demonstrators in 1982.

Democracy in these countries had become an empty shell. Egypt has had only three presidents between 1956 and 2005, and none of them were voted out of office. In Syria, Hafez Assad served as president from 1971 until his death in 2000, and he was succeeded by his son Bashar.

Saddam Hussein

The abandonment of democracy was most severe in Iraq. After the Ba'athists finally came to power in 1968, they immediately began destroying all real and potential opponents. At the direction of the new head of the **security police**, thirty-one-year-old Saddam Hussein, thousands of people were imprisoned, tortured, and killed. Later, during the eleven-year presidency of Ahmad Hassan al-Bakr, it was his deputy Saddam who held the real power. After al-Bakr's resignation in 1979, Saddam became president. Any opposition was crushed, often with appalling cruelty. The Ba'ath Party ceased to function as a political party in the normal sense. It became an organization for explaining, implementing, and enforcing Saddam's policies.

Educating the Young

"Teach students to object to their parents if they hear them discussing state secrets, and to warn them that this is not correct. Teach them to criticize their mothers and fathers, respectfully, if they hear them talking about organizational and Ba'ath Party secrets. You must place a son of the revolution with a trustworthy eye and firm mind in every corner, and teach him to object, with respect, to either of his parents should he discover them wasting the state's wealth, which he should let them know is dearer than his own . . . ."

Extract from a speech by Saddam Hussein to a mass meeting of Iraqi Ministry of Education employees in 1976. Children, he insisted, must be taught that loyalty to the Ba'ath Party, and himself, comes before loyalty to their families. As quoted in Kanan Makiya's Republic of Fear *[Berkeley: University of California Press, 1998].*

Religious Governments

Saudi Arabia

Since the establishment of the Arab Islamic empire in the seventh century, politics and religion in the Middle East have often gone hand in hand. Many tribal, national, and imperial leaders have taken on the role of both political and religious leadership. When these roles have been separated, political and religious leaders have usually established a mutually supportive relationship.

The creation of Saudi Arabia was an important example of such collaboration. In the eighteenth century, the Saud family made an alliance with a new **Sunni Muslim** sect, the Wahhabists. This sect took a fundamentalist approach to Islam. Followers took the teachings of the Prophet Muhammad literally and sought to undo the changes that Islam had undergone since his time.

When the new state of Saudi Arabia was established in 1932,

This photograph from 1942 shows King Ibn Saud. Between 1902 and 1932, his armies conquered the territories that now form the modern state of Saudi Arabia.

Sharia

Sharia is a system of rules and laws that derive from the Islamic holy book, the Koran, and the books of hadith, as interpreted by generations of Islamic religious scholars. In recent decades, the implementation of sharia has spread. It now forms the basis of the legal systems in Saudi Arabia, Iran, Pakistan, and other smaller Muslim countries. Many Muslims have welcomed this new institutionalization of traditional Muslim values, but many others see a strict adherence to sharia as restrictive and undemocratic, particularly where the rights of women are concerned.

Wahhabism was proclaimed as the state's official religion. It has remained so ever since. Its rules and principles are supposed to govern the behavior of both citizens and guests and are enforced by a special religious police. These rules are, by Western standards, very restrictive, especially to women. They are resented by many Saudi citizens, particularly when members of the ruling family are sometimes seen to flout them with impunity.

The Turn to Islam

In other Middle Eastern countries such as Egypt, Syria, Iraq, and Iran, the mixing of politics and religion was frequently seen —by both rulers and ruled—as an obstacle to progress. Arab and Iranian nationalists looked to the example of the United States and Europe, where the separation of politics and religion had opened the way to centuries of economic and political progress. In Egypt and Syria, religious parties like the **Muslim Brotherhood** were persecuted and outlawed. In Iran, both shahs believed that weakening the power of the Islamic clergy was an essential step on the road to modernization.

By the 1970s, however, it was becoming clear that this **secular**, one-party approach to politics was failing to provide the promised progress. Many Arabs and Iranians started wondering whether separating religion and politics was such a good idea. Perhaps, some thought, Islam could provide the answer to the region's political, economic, and social problems.

In most countries, these Islamists remained a significant minority, but in one country—Iran—they proved numerous enough to seize power and to establish an Islamic government.

The Iranian Revolution

Among the countries of the Middle East, Iran has suffered the most violent swings between **Westernization** and **Islamization**. In the 1930s, the pro-Western Reza Shah tried to force Western values, dress, and behavior on his often unwilling people. This ensured him and his son, Muhammad Reza Shah Pahlavi, of the Iranian clergy's bitter opposition. When, early in the 1950s, the second shah found himself involved in a bitter dispute with his nationalist parliament, the clergy supported the nationalists. In 1979, it was an alliance of these two groups—the pro-democratic secular nationalists and the antisecular clergy—that overthrew the shah.

Once the shah was gone, however, the alliance fell apart. The two groups had such different visions for Iran's future that compromise proved impossible. The Islamists created their own institutions—local parties (the neighborhood committees), courts (the revolutionary tribunals), and armed forces (the revolutionary guards corps). From 1980–1982, they fought and won a virtual **civil war** with the forces of the prodemocratic secular nationalists. After the Islamist victory, the institutions of the state continued to exist, but real power rested with the Islamists and the institutions they had set up. In Iran's new **Islamic Republic**, the religious leadership gave the orders to the political leadership.

No Hiding Place

"[In the West] what [an individual] wants to do in the privacy of his home, drinking wine, gambling, or other such dirty deeds, the government has nothing to do with him. Only if he comes out screaming, then he would be prosecuted, because that disturbs the peace. . . . Islam and divine (Godly) governments are not like that. These [governments] have commandments for everybody, everywhere, at any place, in any condition. If a person were to commit an immoral dirty deed right next to his house, Islamic governments have business with him."

Ayatollah Khomeini, explaining his account of the difference between Islamic and Western-style government, as quoted in Sandra Mackey's The Iranians *[New York: Plume, 1998].*

The Grand Mufti of Jerusalem

Hajj Muhammad Amin al Husseini was an important Arab leader in Palestine between the world wars. Born into a prominent religious family, he became the leader of an Arab nationalist group in Jerusalem after World War I. In 1920, the British sentenced Husseini to fifteen years in prison for organizing anti-Jewish violence but then decided they had a better use for him. Eager to increase their popularity among the Palestinian Arabs, they gave Husseini the position of Grand Mufti—or chief religious judge—of Jerusalem. From this position of religious and political authority, the Grand Mufti encouraged Arab opposition to Jewish immigration and played a key role in the Arab revolt of the late 1930s. During World War II, he collaborated with Hitler's Germany in the hope that a Nazi victory would see both Jews and British expelled from Palestine.

Hajj Muhammad Amin al Husseini, former Mufti of Jerusalem, in talks with Nazi leader Adolf Hitler during World War II. Al Husseini had fled the Middle East after taking part in revolts against the British in both Palestine and Iraq.

The Islamic Republic

The Iranian constitution created in 1979 reflected the dominance of the clergy. Like most secular constitutions, it established an elected parliament (a new *Majlis*) and president, but it granted the final word on any matter to the highest religious body (the Council of Guardians) and the supreme religious leader (the *faqih*). The Majlis could pass whatever laws it wanted, but the Council of Guardians could veto any laws that it considered contrary to Islam. And the council itself could be overruled by the faqih.

In the ten years that followed the revolution, both the Islamic Republic and the first faqih, Ayatollah Khomeini, enjoyed the support of most Iranians. The religious leaders

Iranian soldiers carry posters of Ayatollah Khomeini during the 1979 revolution. The armed forces' refusal to defend the shah played a crucial part in his overthrow.

were generally thought to be honest, even by those who opposed their ideas. Since Khomeini's death in 1989, however, accusations of **corruption** have multiplied. Many Iranians now believe that a significant number of religious leaders have used their position to enrich themselves.

In the meantime, the problems associated with running a modern state have split the clergy into two general camps. The first of these camps, the "hardliners," includes clergy who are opposed to any weakening of the revolution's Islamic character. The "pragmatists," in the second camp, are more willing to relax the rules when they get in the way of Iran's economic efficiency. Elections allow Iranians to influence the contest between these two groups, although the clergy bars certain candidates. In June 2005 a hardliner, Mahmoud Ahmadinejad, was elected president. His determination to pursue a nuclear energy program and his anti-Semitic statements have caused concern in the West.

Half a Man

"There is a place a mere five hours' flight from where I sit writing this book where I have a price, and that price is that of just half a man.

There is another world, a strange world where a man can kill me and escape execution unless my family pays to top up my worth to the price of a man.

If my father should die in this other world, I inherit one share to every two shares my brother gets. And if my husband dies, I can expect only one-eighth of the life we built together.

There is a place, just five hours from here, where sons belong to their mother for only the first seven years of their lives.

There is a place where I am only half a witness in its courts.

There is a place where I need my father's permission to marry, no matter what my age.

There is a place where I need my husband's consent to get a passport and his agreement before I can travel.

There is a place, just five hours' flight from here, where I am but half a man."

Iranian-born journalist Cherry Mosteshar, writing in England, where she was raised and educated, about the situation of women in Iran's Islamic Republic. Quoted from her book Unveiled *[London: Hodder & Stoughton, 1995].*

CHAPTER 5

Democracy in the Middle East

In the early years of the twenty-first century, there has been much discussion of the need for more democracy in the Middle East. Democratic governments, many Middle Easterners argue, are more likely to give their people what they want. Democracies, many outsiders argue, are more likely to be stable and peaceful. Everyone will benefit.

The Ingredients of Democracy

What are the ingredients of a real democracy? Some are fairly obvious. All adults, male and female, should be able to vote at

An Israeli from the extreme right-wing Moledet party takes part in a demonstration in 2002 aimed at occupying Jerusalem's Temple Mount. The site is considered holy by both Muslims and Jews.

Yasser Arafat was a controversial leader. To his supporters, he helped raise Palestinian hopes of independence. To his critics, he was a **terrorist** and an obstacle to Palestinian democracy.

"... putting an end to [our people's] feelings of being wronged and of having suffered an historic injustice is the strongest guarantee to achieve coexistence and openness between our two peoples and future generations. Our two peoples are awaiting today this historic hope, and they want to give peace a real chance."

Yasser Arafat (left), president of the Palestinian National Authority, speaking at the White House in 1993, at the signing of a partial peace with Israeli Prime Minister Yitzhak Rabin. Rabin was assassinated two years later, and Arafat died in 2004.

regular intervals for the government of their choice. Their votes should be cast in a **secret ballot**, so that no pressure can be put on an individual to vote a certain way. The voting process and the counting of votes should be overseen by an independent authority, not the existing government.

There should be a real choice between distinct political parties and programs. Those parties should be allowed to operate freely and to get their message across to the people. The electorate—the people—should have knowledge and information to make a reasonable choice. Since a free press and media are obviously crucial in both respects, these entities should neither be run by the government nor completely controlled by the rich and powerful.

Democracy should not involve merely electing a government to represent the people who voted for it. A democratic government is supposed to represent all the people, not just its own supporters. If it fails to do this, it becomes a tyranny of the majority. The only real protection against this is for citizens to have clearly-defined rights as individuals that cannot be overturned by the country's leaders.

This is a difficult list of ingredients to gather together, and many Western governments that consider themselves democracies are missing several of them. Over the last fifty years, most governments in the Middle Eastern countries have struggled to secure any of these ingredients for democracy.

Elections in Egypt and Iran

The elections that took place in Egypt and Iran during 2005 offer good examples of how far these countries are from real democracy. In Egypt, much stress was placed on the fact that President Hosni Mubarak was facing opposition candidates for the first time. In all the other elections of his twenty-four-year rule, the Egyptian people had been given the simple choice of

Six years after the end of Lebanon's civil war, two Lebanese children walk to school through the ruins of Beirut. During the war, the skyscraper in the distance was a favorite haunt of snipers.

Democracy in Lebanon

The borders of Lebanon were drawn by the French in 1920 to create a country with a narrow Christian majority. In 1943, when Lebanon became independent, it was agreed that Christians would have six seats in the Lebanese Parliament for every five that the Muslims had. The same 6:5 ratio was applied to posts in the country's civil service, its judicial system, and its military. This system of dividing political power between religious groups is called **confessionalism**.

Over the next thirty years, the Christians used their built-in majority to seize unfair political and economic advantages. During the same period, because the Muslim birth rate was substantially higher than that of the Christians, the Christian majority standing disappeared. Muslim anger over their continued unequal treatment, and the Christian refusal to accept changes despite the population shift, were the main causes of the Lebanese Civil War (1975–1991). In 1989, a new agreement was set out in the National Reconciliation Charter. From that year on, parliamentary seats would be divided equally between the two communities.

"yes" or "no" to his continued presidency.

Despite the apparent widening of choice, the election in 2005 was condemned as unfair by both opposition candidates and outside observers. Before the election took place, Mohammed Habib, the spokesman for the main opposition party, the Muslim Brotherhood, claimed that "the authorities have already got the ballot boxes ready with the votes inside, and they are deciding whether it would look better internationally if Mubarak wins with 75 percent or 80 percent of the vote" (quoted in the *Independent*, July 9, 2005). After the election was over, allegations of vote buying, violent intimidation, and government use of government vehicles to carry its supporters to the polls were widespread. Further, the commission appointed to oversee the election process was appointed by the government.

In the Iranian election, the two main candidates for the presidency did offer voters a real choice, and the vote itself was conducted fairly. The failure of Iranian democracy occurred before and after the actual election. Before the election, the list of candidates was limited to those whom the country's religious rulers found acceptable. After the election, the victorious candidate, Mahmoud Ahmadinejad, found his freedom of action restricted by those same religious rulers.

Iraq

The original reasons given for the American-led invasion of Iraq in 2003 were Saddam Hussein's possession of **weapons of mass destruction** and the need to remove him as part of the **War on Terror**. When it became clear that Iraq had no weapons of mass destruction and that invading Iraq had made winning the War on Terror more difficult, a third reason for the invasion was emphasized: Iraq would be turned into a democracy. As such, it would provide an example for the rest of the Middle East to follow.

Two years after the overthrow of Iraqi dictator Saddam Hussein, U.S. troops from the 3rd Infantry Division gather outside one of Baghdad's bombed-out presidential palaces for a change of command ceremony.

The problems involved in achieving this transition are huge. Iraq has three increasingly separate communities—the **Shi'a Muslims**, the Sunni Muslims, and the **Kurds**. As the Shi'as number much more than half of the total population, they are likely to have the most members in any democratic government. Most Shi'as are also in favor of a more Islamic approach to government. The Shi'a leadership knows that most Sunnis and Kurds do not want this sort of government, so they have proposed a highly decentralized system in which the Sunnis and Kurds will be able to look after most of their own affairs. The Kurds have accepted this, but the Sunnis have not. As past leaders of Iraq—under both the British and the Ba'ath—the Sunnis are reluctant to accept a minor role in the new Iraq, particularly when theirs is the only region in the country that has no oil.

A further complication is the growing strength of **Islamic fundamentalists** in Iraq. Most of these fundamentalists are Iraqis, although some have come from abroad. Some groups have connections with the international terrorist organization al-Qaeda. All of them reject democracy as a Western idea and are doing everything they can to sabotage its introduction into Iraq. They would prefer a strict Islamic Republic and a policy of zero tolerance toward anything they consider un-Islamic.

Israel

Israel is certainly the most democratic country in the region. Its regular elections are fairly conducted and offer Israelis a real choice of alternative governments. Its media are free and open, and its **judiciary** operates independently of government.

Some critics say that Israel lacks several of the ingredients of a true democracy. Israel was created as a Jewish country, and most of its Jewish majority clearly wish it to remain as such. About 20 percent of Israelis are not Jews. An Israeli Jew has the right to have his entire family come and live in Israel, but an Israeli Arab does not have that right. Israel's Basic Law on Human Dignity and Liberty and the country's system of proportional representation, however, protect the individual rights of all of its citizens and allow their votes to count in choosing the country's leaders.

CHAPTER 6

Foreign Interference

Since the Macedonian Alexander the Great conquered most of the Middle East in the fourth century B.C., the governments and leaders of the region have had to put up with foreign

U.S. President Franklin D. Roosevelt (on the right) meets with Saudi Arabia's King Ibn Saud. The conference was held aboard the USS *Quincy*, in Egypt's Great Bitter Lake, in February 1945. Roosevelt wanted to extend American influence in the Middle East.

interference and pressure. Over the last hundred years, this interference and these pressures have intensified. Outsiders have constantly meddled in the affairs of the Middle East, protecting some of its governments and leaders and undermining others.

Supporting Dictators

During the mandate period, Britain protected the constitutional monarchies it had installed in Egypt, Transjordan, and Iraq from local nationalists and democrats. During the **Cold War**, the American-led West helped keep Egyptian presidents Sadat and Mubarak in power by providing enormous financial and military support. The Soviet Union did the same for Nasser's Egypt and Hafez Assad's Syria. The American alliance with Saudi Arabia ensured the survival of the Saud family dictatorship: when the kingdom was threatened by Iraq's occupation of neighboring Kuwait in 1990, U.S. troops were sent immediately to defend it. The American alliance with the shah of Iran proved less successful. When he was overthrown by his own people in 1979, the United States switched its support to Iran's traditional enemy, Saddam Hussein's Iraq.

All these examples of foreign interference were antidemocratic. In each case, Western powers ensured or tried to ensure the survival of governments and leaders who had no interest in ruling democratically or promoting democracy. This pattern of Western behavior was noticed by the peoples of the Middle East.

Antidemocracy

"We have declared a bitter war against democracy and all those who seek to enact it. Democracy is . . . based on the right to choose your religion, [and that is] against the rule of God. . . . Whoever helps promote this and all those candidates, as well as the voters, are also part of this, and are considered enemies of God."

From a videotape attributed to Abu Musab al-Zarqawi, who led al-Qaeda in Iraq until he was killed in June 2006. As taken from CNN internet report, January 23, 2005.

Three Leaders

The unpopularity of Western governments and policies in the Middle East had another important effect besides making Middle Easterners suspicious of democracy. Several of the Arab and Iranian leaders who became popular throughout the region were those who stood up to the West. Egypt's President Nasser failed to create a democracy, kick-start the Egyptian economy, or destroy Israel, but his defiance of the West during the Suez Crisis of 1956 made him an Arab hero. The Ayatollah Khomeini was, to many Middle Easterners, a religious extremist, but his description of the United States as "the Great Satan" struck a chord throughout the Middle

U.S. Secretary of State Condoleezza Rice meets with Iraqi Kurdish leader Massoud Barzani in May 2005. Massoud Barzani is the son of Mustafa Barzani, who is pictured with Saddam Hussein on page 20.

Prodemocracy

"We should all look to a future when every government respects the will of its citizens—because the ideal of democracy is universal. For sixty years, my country, the United States, pursued stability at the expense of democracy in this region here in the Middle East—and we achieved neither. Now, we are taking a different course. We are supporting the democratic aspirations of all people. . . .

We know these advances will not come easily, or all at once. We know that different societies will find forms of democracy that work for them. When we talk about democracy, though, we are referring to governments that protect certain basic rights for all their citizens—among these, the right to speak freely. The right to associate. The right to worship as you wish. The freedom to educate your children—boys and girls. And freedom from the midnight knock of the secret police.

Securing these rights is the hope of every citizen, and the duty of every government. In my own country, the progress of democracy has been long and difficult . . . it was only in my lifetime that my government guaranteed the right to vote for all of its people. . . . Here in the Middle East, that same long hopeful process of democratic change is now beginning to unfold. Millions of people are demanding freedom for themselves and democracy for their countries."

U.S. Secretary of State Condoleezza Rice, speaking at the American University in Cairo on June 10, 2005.

East. Saddam Hussein mixed incompetence with barbarity, but to many Arabs he was the only leader prepared to take on the Americans.

Although these three influential leaders became popular in part by opposing the West, iron-fisted policies at home also played a role in keeping them in power. In spite of their opposition to colonialism, Western support of family dictatorships, unfair oil deals, and Israel, this did little to bring peace and prosperity to their countries.

The U.S. Dilemma

In 2005, U.S. Secretary of State Condoleezza Rice said that America had, in the past, been too concerned with stability in the Middle East and not concerned enough with democracy. The context of this statement was important. At the time, the United States was justifying the occupation of Iraq by saying that it was preparing that country for democracy. The Americans were also hoping that a successful transition to democracy in Iraq would encourage similar transitions elsewhere in the Middle East. The administration of George W. Bush claimed that more and better democracies in the Middle East would be in everyone's interest.

Many experts on the Middle East disputed this view. They predicted that free elections would only produce secular governments in a small minority of Middle Eastern countries. In most of them, free elections would produce Islamist governments of varying strictness. The only things these secular and Islamist governments would have in common would be their anti-Israeli and anti-American attitudes. They would be less reliable suppliers of oil than the current family dictatorships.

U.S. policy toward the Middle East is caught in the middle. If the United States continues to support unpopular regimes and pursue policies that many Middle Easterners regard as anti-Islamic, then those regimes may be overthrown. If it insists on the introduction of democracy, then those regimes will probably be turned out by elections. Faced with this choice, the United States may decide to continue its support for pro-Western governments that look like democracies, but which really are not. This was the policy that Britain pursued between the 1920s and 1950s, with disastrous results.

A Better Way

Western interference in the Middle East will continue as long as Middle Eastern oil remains essential to the functioning of the world economy. But that interference need not prove as damaging as it has been over the past century.

The Middle East is awash with grievances, many of them justified. If these are addressed, then the numbers of people willing to join or support the terrorists will eventually diminish. The people of the Middle East, like people everywhere else, want economic progress, governments that listen to them, respect for their cherished traditions, and an end to foreign interference. If these goals seem reachable, Islamic fundamentalism will lose much of its attraction.

Western involvement in pursuit of goals such as these would be constructive. A just solution to the Israeli-Palestinian conflict, for example, is only possible with Western diplomatic and economic help. More assistance to the oil-poor Arab countries would help to mop up the unemployment that helps breed resentment. More pressure for controlled change on the family dictators might prevent their kingdoms from exploding. Peace, prosperity, and justice offer considerably more hope of lasting stability than fake democracies and much less ammunition for the terrorists.

An Iraqi at work in one of the country's northern oil fields, early in 2004. Three years after the war began, Iraqi oil production was still far below pre-war levels.

CHAPTER 7

Future Prospects

The quality of Middle Eastern governments and leaders matters. It matters to the peoples of the Middle East who suffer the consequences of corrupt, undemocratic, and incompetent government. It matters to the rest of the world, which has seen the region degenerate into an increasingly uncertain source of oil and a breeding ground for international terrorism. So what are the prospects? There are reasons for both optimism and pessimism.

Reasons for Pessimism

The reasons for pessimism about the region's future can be grouped under the following five well-known topics: oil depletion, the war in Iraq, regional consequences of the war in Iraq, Iran's nuclear program (and the reaction to it), and finally, the Israeli-Palestinian conflict.

First, as world oil supplies start to dwindle, the importance of the Middle East—which contains roughly two-thirds of the world's proven **oil reserves**—is bound to increase. The need to guarantee regular supplies is likely to result in increasing foreign interference. This in turn may provoke anti-Western feeling and increase support for international terrorism.

Second, for many, it is hard to imagine a successful resolution of the current conflict in Iraq. On the one hand, the country's history and ethnic-religious patchwork make it difficult to devise a settlement acceptable to all three main communities—the Shi'a Arabs, Sunni Arabs, and Kurds. On the other hand, resistance to the occupation will continue until Iraq's independence is returned. Even with formation of a new Iraqi government, some believe resistance will last as long as the United States maintains its current plans to establish a permanent economic and military presence in the country.

Israeli prime minister, Ariel Sharon, discussing the re-housing of settlers evacuated from the Gaza Strip in August 2005. After suffering a massive stroke in January 2006, Sharon was replaced as prime minister by Ehud Olmert as the leader of the new Kadima party.

A third reason for pessimism is the regional fallout from conflicts. One consequence of the war in Iraq has been a growth of support for Islamic fundamentalism, in both that country and the region as a whole. This will make the task of spreading democracy much harder.

The fourth matter is Iran's plans to create a nuclear energy program. These plans—which may or may not include secret plans to acquire nuclear weapons—offer another potential source of conflict. The fact that Iran's major critics—the United States, Britain, and Israel—all have nuclear weapons of their own is not lost on either Iranians or their fellow Middle Easterners. An attempt to take military action against Iran may unify the country behind its hard-line leadership, strengthening those in the Iranian leadership who are most opposed to democracy.

A final matter facing the region is the Israeli-Palestinian conflict. This conflict has created more anti-Western resentment among Middle Eastern Muslims than all the other conflicts put together. The Palestinian National Authority will not be able to restrain its people from attacking Israel without the offer of a reasonable peace. The Israeli government will not offer a reasonable peace until its people feel safe from attack. Since the death of Yasser Arafat, the Palestinian leader, in 2004, **Hamas** (the main Islamist movement in the Palestinian territories) began to win more support among the Palestinian people. In January 2006, Hamas was elected to form the majority government. Hamas opposes peace with Israel, making the conflict seem as intractable as ever.

Reasons for Optimism

On the positive side, the pressures for greater democracy are mounting throughout the region. In oil-poor countries like Egypt and Syria, people's patience with one-party countries and presidents-for-life is running out. Recent elections have been less than free and fair, but at least they have been held.

There have also been some tentative steps toward democracy in the family dictatorships. In most of the Gulf, advisory councils have been elected, with promises of more to follow. In Saudi Arabia, a **consultative council** has been created. None of these councils has any real power, but at least its members have opportunities to speak their minds. In those countries where women are still denied the right to vote, there is increasing pressure for this to change.

Much of the pressure for greater democracy comes from within the Middle East, but outside developments are also playing a part. The drive by the United States to democratize

A group of Iraqis raise their purple index fingers, showing that they have just cast their votes in the December 2005 elections.

Debating Iraq's Future

"Sheikh Mohammed al-Yacobi told the *Guardian*: 'Ninety-eight percent of the people are Muslims. The Iraqi constitution must not commit to anything that will go against sharia [Islamic law].'

Sheikh Mohammed al-Tabatabi told worshipers: 'The West calls for freedom and liberty. Islam is not calling for this. Islam rejects such liberty. True liberty is obedience to God and to be liberated from desires. The danger we should anticipate in the coming days is the danger to our religion from the West trying to spread pornographic magazines and channels.'

Under Saddam, Iraq was a secular society. Women had equal rights with men and freedom to dress in Western clothes. It was more lax than many of its neighbors about alcohol. But Sheikh Tabatabi said: 'We will not allow shops to sell alcohol. . . .' He added that women should not be allowed to wander unveiled around Qadhimaya City.

A third cleric, Quais al-Khazaaly, said: 'I think the right decision is to have an Islamist state. If the United States blocks such a state and people want it, this will lead to lots of trouble with the United States.'"

The opinions of three prominent religious leaders in Iraq. They illustrate the difficulty of reconciling Islam and democracy. Taken from a report in British newspaper, the Guardian, *March 5, 2003.*

the Middle East may be self-interested. It may not work in Iraq. But it is putting pressure on regimes to make changes. The growth of the Internet is also making it harder for the family and one-party dictatorships to keep their people in ignorance.

Perhaps the best reason for feeling optimistic about the spread of democratic governments and leaders in the Middle East is the absence of a real alternative. Over the last fifty years, secular one-party countries, family dictatorships, and Islamic fundamentalism have all proved incapable of giving the people of the region the political and economic progress they want.

1914–1918 World War I.

1917 Balfour Declaration.

1920 Britain given mandates to rule Palestine, Transjordan, and Iraq; France given mandate to rule Syria (including future Lebanon). Nationalist uprising against British rule erupts in Iraq.

1922 Egypt is given formal independence.

1932 Iraq is given formal independence.

1939–1945 World War II.

1945–1947 Violence escalates in Palestine.

1947 United Nations (UN) partitions Palestine.

1947–1948 Fighting in Palestine.

1948 State of Israel is founded.

1948–1949 First Arab-Israeli War.

1950s Arab guerrillas mount raids into Israel from Egypt.

1951–1953 Conflict between Iranian Prime Minister Mossadegh and the Western powers ends with Mossadegh's overthrow.

1952 Free Officer revolution in Egypt.

1956 Nasser's nationalization of the Suez Canal sparks the Suez Crisis.

1958 Iraqi officers overthrow pro-British regime in Baghdad.

1960 Organization of Petroleum Exporting Countries (OPEC) is founded.

1962–1967 War of independence in Aden Protectorate (South Yemen).

1962–1970 Civil war in North Yemen.

1963–1975 Civil war in Oman.

1967 (June) Second Arab-Israeli War.

1970 Black September in Jordan.

1973 (October) Third Arab-Israeli War.

1974 Yasser Arafat makes "Gun or Olive Branch" speech in New York.

1975–1991 Lebanese Civil War.

1977 Menachem Begin becomes prime minister of Israel.

1978–1996 Afghan civil wars.

1979 (January) Iranian revolution. (March) Peace treaty between Egypt and Israel. (June) Saddam Hussein becomes president of Iraq. (December) Soviets intervene in Afghanistan.

1979–1980 Libyan forces mount military interventions in Chad and Tunisia.

1980–1982 Virtual civil war in Iran.

1980–1988 Iran-Iraq War.

1982 Israel invades Lebanon.

1987–1988 Osama bin Laden founds al-Qaeda.

1987–1993 First intifada.

1990 Iraq invades Kuwait; Osama bin Laden's offer of military assistance is rejected by the Saudi Arabian government.

1991 UN coalition forces Iraq out of Kuwait.

1993–1994 Secret talks between Israel and the PLO take place in Oslo, Norway.

1994 Establishment of Palestinian National Authority.

1996 Taliban takes Afghan capital Kabul.

2001 (February) Ariel Sharon becomes prime minister of Israel. (September) 9/11 attacks on the United States; the War on Terror is declared.

2002 President George W. Bush claims there is an "Axis of Evil" that includes Iraq, Iran, and North Korea.

2003 Saddam Hussein is overthrown by United States-led invasion.

2003 Violent resistance to occupation of Iraq occurs.

2005 Israel withdraws settlements from Gaza Strip.

GLOSSARY

absolute power: power without restriction

accountable: having to explain and justify decisions

Arab nationalists: supporters of the movement that advocates development of an increasingly united Arab world

Arabian Peninsula: large area of land surrounded on three sides by the Red Sea, Arabian Sea, and Persian Gulf

assassinated: murdered for political reasons

Ba'ath: a movement organized around set of ideas stressing Arab unity and modernization that led to creation of political parties in several countries including Syria and Iraq

caliph: leader of all Muslims

civil war: war between different groups in the same country

clergy: religious officials

Cold War: the period of hostility between the free-enterprise capitalist and communist worlds between 1947 and the late 1980s during which the United States and the Soviet Union competed for influence in other countries but never fell into direct military conflict

colonialism: ruling of economically underdeveloped countries by economically advanced countries

confessionalism: system of arranging political power in Lebanon according to the relative size of the two main communities

constitution: in politics, the way a country is set up to safeguard its fundamental principles

constitutional monarchy: a monarchy in which the elected parliament, and not the monarch, has the final say

consultative council: group of people who can give advice but not actually make decisions

corruption: immoral practices like fraud and bribery

democracy: political system in which governments are regularly elected by the people, or a country in which this system exists

dictator: individual who rules on his or her own, unrestricted by others

emir: Muslim ruler

faqih: supreme religious leader in Iran since the Islamic revolution of 1979

Free Officers Movement: groups of young officers who came together in several Arab countries with the intention of overthrowing corrupt and pro-Western governments

Hamas: a Palestinian militant Islamist organization formed in 1987, at the time of the first Palestinian uprising against Israel's occupation in the West Bank and Gaza. Hamas is widely considered to be a terrorist organization.

Islam: one of the world's major three monotheistic (one God) religions, founded by the Prophet Muhammad in the seventh century

Islamic fundamentalist: someone who believes in strictly following the rules— or a particular interpretation of the rules— of Islam

Islamic Republic: government that bases its laws on Islamic law

Islamist: someone who wants Islam to play the key role in government and society

Islamization: making society stick more closely to Islamic principles and laws

GLOSSARY

Judaism: one of the world's three major monotheistic (one God) religions (along with Christianity and Islam)

judiciary: system of law and law enforcement

Kurds: Middle Eastern people, mostly Sunni Muslims, who have no state of their own but form large minorities in Turkey, Iraq, and Iran

League of Nations: the international organization founded in 1919 to encourage cooperation among nations and to guarantee them peace and security

mandates: permissions to rule that have been authorized by international agreement

Mesopotamian provinces: the lowlands watered by the Tigris and Euphrates rivers during the time of the Ottoman Empire

modernize: bring up to date with current ideas and technology

Muslim: someone who believes in Islam

Muslim Brotherhood: Islamist group that became powerful in Egypt during the twentieth century

nationalism: devotion to one's own nation, putting it above all others

oil reserves: oil still in the ground

Ottoman Empire: the empire of the Ottoman Turks, which lasted over 600 years (1299–1922), and which included all of the Middle East except Iran and the desert interior of Arabia

Palestinian National Authority: name given to the government of the West Bank and the Gaza Strip

radical: far-reaching or extreme

secret ballot: a vote organized in such a way that no one knows how any particular individual voted

secular: not religious

security police: police concerned with the security of the government in power

shah: Iranian word for "emperor"

Shi'a Muslims: Muslims who believe the rightful leaders of Islam are the descendants of Muhammad's son-in-law Ali

Suez Crisis: international crisis that began with Egypt's nationalization of the Suez Canal in July 1956. The crisis involved Israeli, British, and French attacks on Egypt in October of that year.

sultan: Muslim ruler

Sunnis Muslims: Muslims who accept the first four caliphs as rightful leaders of Islam

terrorist: a person who uses violence to intimidate people for political reasons

Wahhabism: the strict form of Islam practiced in Saudi Arabia

War on Terror: a worldwide campaign to eliminate terrorism that began in September 2002, after the terrorist attacks on the United States on September 11, 2001

weapons of mass destruction: weapons—such as nuclear, chemical, and biological weapons—that are capable of killing thousands of people with a single blow

Westernization: adoption of Western ideas, technologies, and cultural values

FURTHER RESOURCES

Web Sites

BBC News: Middle East
  http://news.bbc.co.uk/1/hi/world/middle_east/default.stm
CNN International: World/Middle East
  http://edition.cnn.com/WORLD/meast/archive
Global Connections: the Middle East
  http://www.pbs.org/wgbh/globalconnections/mideast
History in the News: Middle East
  http://www.albany.edu/history/middle-east/

Note to educators and parents: The publisher has carefully reviewed these Web sites to ensure that they are suitable for children. Many Web sites change frequently, however, and Gareth Stevens, Inc., cannot guarantee that a site's future contents will continue to meet our high standards of quality and educational value. Be advised that children should be closely supervised whenever they access the Internet.

Books

Greenfield, Howard. *A Promise Fulfilled: Theodor Herzl, Cherim Weizmann, David Ben-Gurion, and the Creation of the State of Israel.* Greenwillow, 2005.

Kras, Sarah Louise. *Anwar Sadat* (Major World Leaders). Chelsea House Publications, 2002.

Stewart, Gail. *Saddam Hussein* (Heroes and Villans). Lucent Books, 2004.

Wagner, Heather Lehr. *King Abdullah II* (Major World Leaders). Chelsea House Publications, 2005.

Woolf, Alex. *The Arab-Israeli Conflict* (Atlas of Conflicts). World Almanac Library, 2005.

ABOUT THE AUTHOR

David Downing has been writing books for adults and children about political, military, and cultural history for thirty years. He has written several books on the modern Middle East. He has lived in the United States and traveled extensively in Asia, Africa, and Latin America. He now resides in Britain.

ABOUT THE CONSULTANT

William Ochsenwald is Professor of History at Virginia Polytechnic Institute and State University. He is author of *The Middle East: A History*, a textbook now in its sixth edition. Professor Ochsenwald has also written many other books and articles dealing with the history of the Middle East.

INDEX